The Great Big
SEARCH and FIND
Activity Book

QED

Contents

Can you spot
these things?

apple core   sun cream

bowl of food   duck

Welcome to the World!

There's lots to see. Come and have a look!

North America

South America

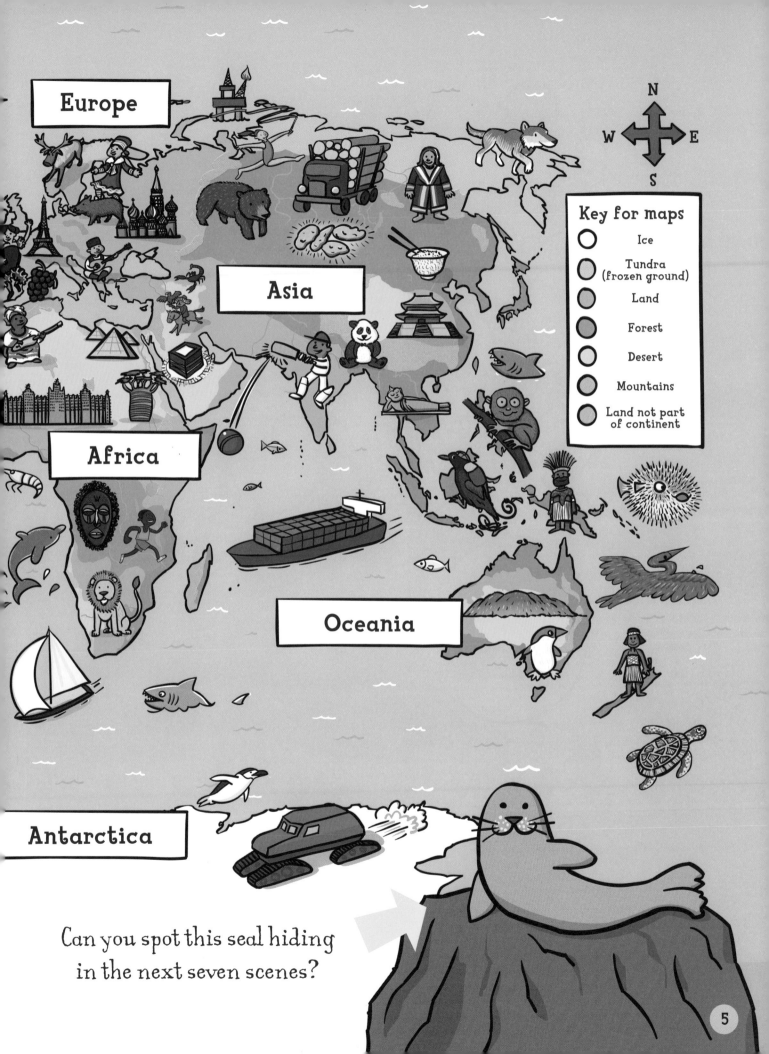

Europe

Asia

Africa

Oceania

Antarctica

N
W E
S

Key for maps
- ◯ Ice
- ◯ Tundra (frozen ground)
- ◯ Land
- ● Forest
- ◯ Desert
- ◯ Mountains
- ● Land not part of continent

Can you spot this seal hiding in the next seven scenes?

5

The Caribbean

Dominican Republic

Puerto Rico

Trinidad and Tobago

Cuba

Jamaica Haiti

Honduras

Nicaragua

Belize

Panama

Costa Rica

Guatemala

El Salvador

Mexico

PACIFIC OCEAN

There are ice fields in the far north and hot rainforests in the south.

North America is the only continent that has every type of climate.

Can you spot these things?

Golden Gate Bridge

moose

ox and cart

beaver

piñata

cactus

South America

Over a third of South America is covered by dripping green rainforest.

Venezuela

Guyana

Suriname

French Guiana

Colombia

Ecuador

Peru

Bolivia

Brazil

8

Europe

Europe has more than 50 countries. It includes the world's smallest country, Vatican City State, and half of the world's biggest country, Russia.

Iceland

United Kingdom

Ireland

Netherlands

NORTH ATLANTIC OCEAN

Belgium

Luxembourg

France

Switzerland

Portugal

Spain

Monaco

Andorra

Can you spot these things?

daffodil

lynx

waffle

racing car

salamander

Africa

NORTH ATLANTIC
OCEAN

Morocco

Western Sahara

Mauritania

Cape
Verde — Senegal

The Gambia

Guinea-Bissau

Guinea

Sierra Leone

Liberia

Côte
d'Ivoire

Ghana

Togo

Benin

Equatorial
Guinea

Gabon

Tunisia

Libya

Algeria

Mali

Niger

Chad

Burkina
Faso

Nigeria

Central Af...
Repu...

Cameroon

Congo

Angola

Namibia

Can you spot these things?

drum   elephant   penguin

gerbil   waterfall

SOUTH ATLANTIC
OCEAN

12

Asia

Can you spot these things?

- Marco Polo sheep
- tarsier
- orangutan
- coffee
- camel
- scorpion

Georgia
Azerbaijan
Kazakhstan
Turkey
Armenia
Uzbekistan
Lebanon
Israel
Syria
Jordan
Turkmenistan
Kyrgyzstan
Tajikistan
Iraq
Iran
Afghanistan
Kuwait
United Arab Emirates
Pakistan
Nepal
Bahrain
Qatar
Saudi Arabia
India
Yemen
Oman
Maldives
Sri Lanka

Oceania

Papua New Guinea

INDIAN OCEAN

GREAT BARRIER REEF

Australia

Tasmania

Many of Australia's animals don't live wild on any other continent.

Can you spot these things?

kiwi fruit   didgeridoo   headdress   sheep   platypus

Nauru

Kiribati

Solomon Islands

Tuvalu

PACIFIC OCEAN

Tokelau

Wallis and Futuna

Samoa

French Polynesia

Vanuatu

Fiji

Niue

New Caledonia

Tonga

Cook Islands

Oceania is made up of more than 10,000 islands.

New Zealanders love rugby. What's your favourite sport?

New Zealand

The Great Barrier Reef is the only living thing you can see from space!

Antarctica

Halley research station (UK)

Amundsen-Scott research station (USA)

SOUTH POLE

SOUTH PACIFIC OCEAN

SOUTHERN OCEAN

Antarctica is a frozen land mostly covered by ice. Near the centre is the South Pole.

SOUTHERN OCEAN

Antarctica is the driest, windiest and coldest place on Earth.

INDIAN OCEAN

Mawson research station (Australia)

How many boats can you see?

Dumont d'Urville research station (France)

Can you spot these things?

Macaroni penguin

Adélie penguin

Emperor penguin

Chinstrap penguin

Gentoo penguin

Which Brazilian dancer is different?

Find 10 differences between these two globes...

We're on the Move

There's lots to see.
Come and have a look!

Caravan park

Bus

Bicycle lane

Underground

There are lots of ways to get around.
What is your favourite way to travel?

Airport

Harbour

Ferry

Spaghetti junction

Trains

This little mouse is hiding. Can you find it in the next six scenes?

Can you spot these things?

driver   motorcycle   clock   rowing boat   lifeboat

23

Can you spot these things?

blue flag | orange chairs | anchor | life buoy | green car

The world's largest ferries can carry 230 cars and 1,200 passengers!

Have you ever been on a ferry?

Can you spot these things?

sign   traffic cone   helicopter   police car   apple

In some big cities, lots of roads cross over each other – they are called spaghetti junctions. In Shanghai, China, six roads cross over each other in this way.

A caravan is a small
home on wheels that can
be towed behind a car.
A camper van can be driven.

The world's smallest caravan is only
slightly larger than a single bed!

Underground trains run beneath many cities all around the world. They carry millions of people every day.

CENTRAL LINE

DISTRICT LINE

How many windows can you see on this train?

Can you spot these things?

bench   balloon   pram   newspaper   guitar

The world's biggest bus runs in China. It can hold up to 300 passengers.

The world's busiest airport is in Atlanta, Georgia. More than 101 million people pass through it each year.

Did you know that the tips of a plane's wings bend upwards when the plane takes off?

Can you spot these things?

pink suitcase
pilot
crate
passenger
Mexican hat

Which container ship is different?

Find 10 differences between these two traffic scenes...

Watch Out! There are Dinosaurs About

Supersaurus

Triceratops

Stegosaurus

Have fun colouring in Dinosaur Island.
Use lots of colours!

Can you spot this baby *Tyrannosaurus rex* (say *Tie-ran-uh-sore-us rex*) in the next six scenes?

Supersaurus
(say Super-sore-us)
was one of the
biggest dinosaurs.

The giant Supersaurus was as long as
10 elephants standing in a line!

Can you spot these things?

red lizard palm tree cactus feather bones

The name Velociraptor (say *Vell-oss-ee-rap-tor*) means 'speedy robber'. This little dinosaur could run very fast.

All baby dinosaurs – even the really big ones – started life by hatching out of eggs.

Make your own baby dinosaur!

Carefully decorate half of an empty, clean eggshell with felt-tip pens. Make a dinosaur head and neck out of modelling clay. Mark the eyes and mouth with a pencil. Place the dinosaur inside the shell so that its face is peeping out.

Can you find my twin? He looks just like me!

Can you find and colour these things?

dinosaur triplets | spotted egg | frilled dinosaur | spiky tail | baby dinosaur

Have fun colouring in all these dinosaur eggs. Use lots of colours!

Although some dinosaurs ate meat, most were plant eaters.

Can you spot these things?

red fish   fern   pine cone   pink flower   snake

47

Stegosaurus (say *Steg-uh-sore-us*) had huge, bony plates along its back and spikes on its tail that were as long as swords!

How many spikes do I have at the end of my tail?

Have fun colouring in all these stomping dinosaurs!

Can you find and colour these things?

lizard

tree stump

fish

butterfly

eggshell

49

People who hunt for fossils are called paleontologists (say pal-ee-ont-ol-o-jists).

Can you spot these things?

hammer

tape measure

brush

drinks bottle

camera

Which *Velociraptor* is different?

Did You Know?

Of course, Dinosaur Island isn't a real place. Lots of these dinosaurs lived millions of years apart and so they would never have met.

Some of the dinosaurs' closest relatives are still around today. You might see one if you look out of your window. They're birds!

No one is certain what colours dinosaurs were, but we know that some had feathers and most of them had scaly skin.

One of the biggest dinosaurs that we know about is the gigantic *Argentinosaurus* (say *Ar-gen-teen-oh-sore-us*). Maybe someone will discover an even bigger one soon!

Anyone can look for dinosaur fossils. One of the first fossil hunters was a little girl named Mary Anning, who lived in England about 200 years ago.

Creatures of the Ocean

Find out who lives in our watery world.

Whale sharks

Sea horses

Octopuses

Coral reef

Have fun colouring in all the strange creatures of the ocean. Use lots of colours!

Beach

Arctic waters

Dolphins

Strange ocean creatures

Can you find this baby shark hiding in the next six ocean scenes?

Deep sea

Can you find and colour these things?

sea horse   fish   diver   turtle   seal

Whale sharks are the world's biggest fish. They are huge, but harmless to humans.

Can you find and colour
these things?

starfish

clam

anchor

sea cucumber

eel

Sea horses are little
fish with tiny fins
that swim upright
very slowly through
the water.

Some of the most beautiful fish in the world live on the Great Barrier Reef near Australia.

Have fun colouring in this busy Arctic scene. Use lots of colours!

Mmm... tasty fish!

In winter polar bears live on the ice that covers the ocean around the North Pole.

Can you find and
colour these things?

sailboat   whale   reindeer   sleeping   walrus
                                  musk ox

Turtles live in the ocean but lay their eggs on the beach. When the baby turtles hatch, they have to crawl to the sea!

Can you spot these things?

sign

eggs

pelican

pink shell

blue crab

Some ocean creatures look very strange indeed!

Can you spot these things?

blobfish   pufferfish   yeti crab   monkfish   parrot fish

Which sea horse is different?

Find 10 differences between these two underwater scenes...

Crocodiles often sleep with their mouths open. Sometimes little birds fly in and pick meat off their teeth!

Can you find and colour these things?

ladybird   dolphin   bird   crocodile nest   frog

In the treetops live the laziest animals in the jungle. The three-toed sloth can happily sleep for up to 20 hours a day!

Can you spot these things?

shield bug   blue butterfly   iguana   caterpillar   green parrot

Poison dart frogs are beautiful but very dangerous!

Some poison dart frogs have enough poison to kill 10 people!

In the rainy jungle, orangutans hold
leaves over their nests to keep them dry!

Tapirs have hooves and long noses.
The babies have spots and stripes.

Can you spot these things?

log   yellow flowers   vine   white bird   red butterfly

Spots and stripes can help animals to blend in with their surroundings and keep them safe.

Can you spot the baby tapir?

At night some creatures sleep, while others come out to hunt for food.

How many bats can you see?

Can you find and colour these things?

genet

moth

owl

beetle

bush baby

81

Which crocodile is different?

Find 10 differences between these two jungle scenes...

Farm vehicles

Sheep

Wheat

Cows

Stables

Can you find this little
lamb hiding in the next
five farm scenes?

Can you spot these things?

donkey   underpants   mole   spoon   bell

Can you find and colour these things?

cat flower frog kettle shoe

Cock-a-doodle-doo!

There are lots of different farm animals on this farm.

Bread, pasta and cereals are often made from wheat.

Can you spot these things?

watch　　scales　　tyre　　comb　　sock

A sheep's fleecy coat can be used to make wool.

93

Can you find and colour these things?

umbrella   book   trampoline   dragonfly   towel

Which pig is different?

Find 10 differences between these two vegetable patches...

Can you spot this puppy hiding in the next six busy city scenes?

More people live in Tokyo, Japan, than in any other city in the world.

Fire engines have sirens and flashing lights
so people know to move out of their way.

Can you spot these things?

stripy kite

teddy bear

basket

lily pad

bin

ice cream

107

The world's biggest shopping centre is in Dubai, UAE. It has 1,200 shops!

More to Colour

Finish drawing the pictures
using the grid to help you.
Then colour them in!

Did you find me?

Find 10 differences between these two houses...

Marvel at the Museum

There's lots to see. Come and have a look!

Ancient Greeks

Vikings

Masks

Ancient Egyptians

The Americas

Can you spot these things?

mask warrior shield visitor sphinx head

Buried treasure

Ancient Romans

Dinosaurs

Gift shop and café

Can you spot this mummy hiding in the next five museum scenes?

Dinosaur fossils are displayed in museums.
This dinosaur was as long as three buses!

Have fun colouring in the dinosaur rooms!

Have you ever been to a dinosaur museum?

Can you find and colour these things?

sign   notebook   book   shoe   dinosaur egg

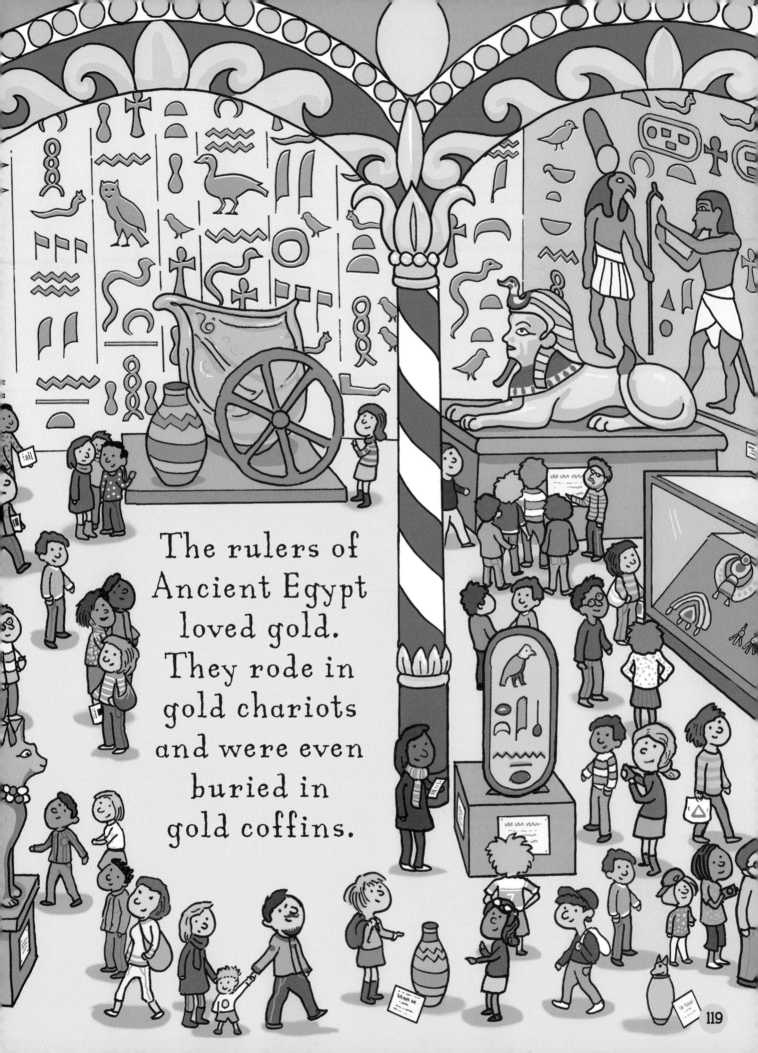

The rulers of Ancient Egypt loved gold. They rode in gold chariots and were even buried in gold coffins.

The Ancient Greeks thought
that art, writing and drama
were very important.

One Ancient Greek story is about a winged horse named Pegasus.

The Ancient Romans loved entertainment. They held parties and feasts at home and went out to see chariot races and gladiator fights.

The Vikings lived more than 1,000 years ago. They travelled to different countries all over Europe in boats called longships.

Which totem pole is different?

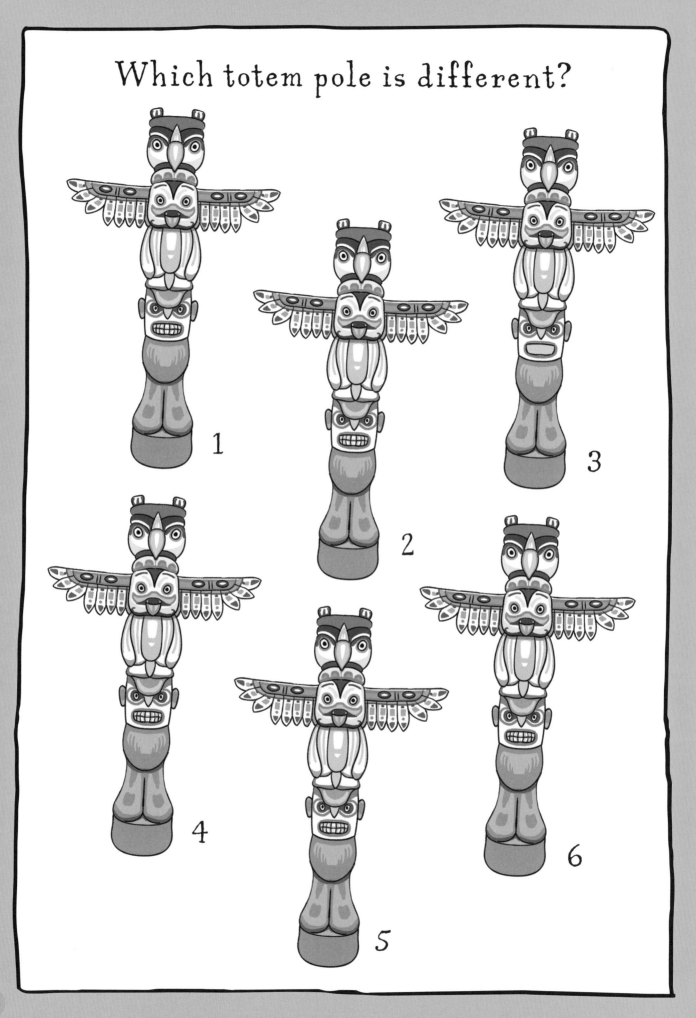

Did You Know?

The word dinosaur comes from the Greek language and means 'terrible lizard'.

Ancient Romans loved eating exotic things such as swans, crows, horses, peacocks and dormice.

The ancient people of Mexico believed in worshipping the Sun to give it enough strength to rise each day.

Some of the first people to wear jewellery were men. They wore chains and bracelets to show how rich they were and to bring them luck in battle.

The Ancient Egyptians invented lots of things we use today, such as paper, pens, locks, keys and even toothpaste!

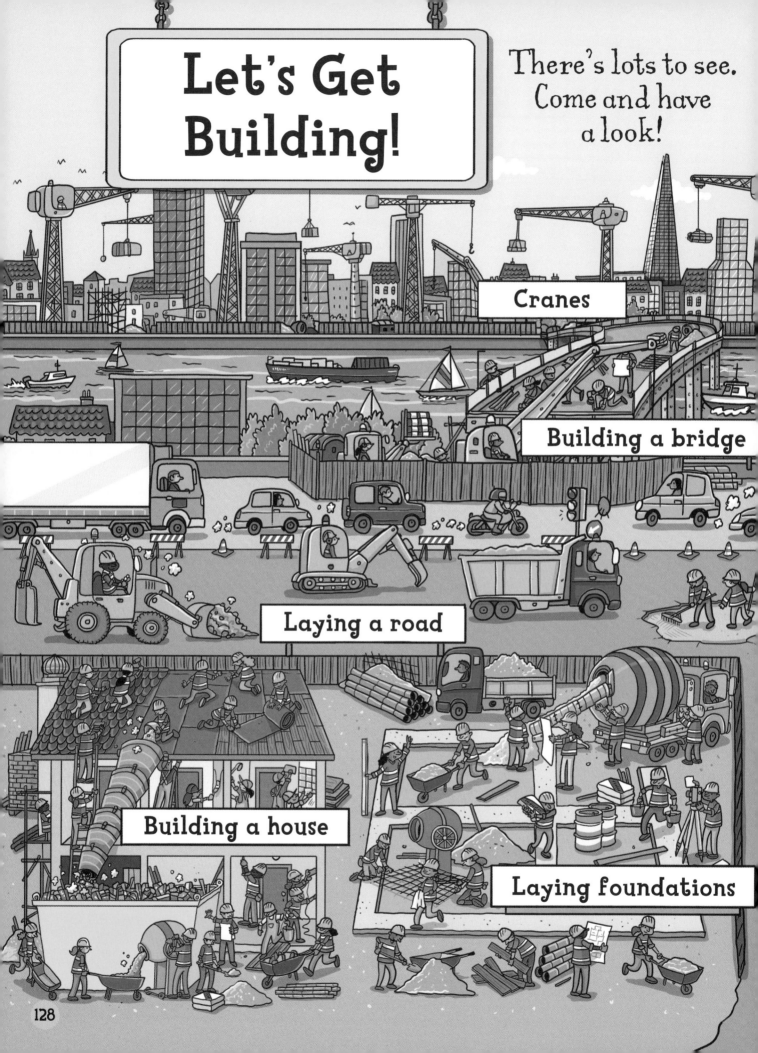

Let's Get Building!

There's lots to see. Come and have a look!

Cranes

Building a bridge

Laying a road

Building a house

Laying foundations

128

Can you spot these things?

 roofer

 oil drums

 builder

builder with wheelbarrow

 green jug

Demolition site

Diggers

Theme park

Playground

Can you spot this bird hiding in the next six scenes?

129

Houses are built on foundations that are dug into the ground. Foundations stop houses from sinking or falling over.

A building site can be dangerous, so builders wear hard hats to keep them safe.

Can you spot these things?

chair

spirit level

hook

flask

wire cutters

131

Can you spot these things?

shower head · screwdriver · pink helmet · cement trowel · hammer

A road is made by laying down layers of sand, stone and concrete. These are pressed down with a heavy roller.

Can you find the heavy roller?

134

Can you spot these things?

rake

spare tyre

traffic lights

red flag

pneumatic drill

Can you spot these things?

blue power drill   kayak   plans   buoy   aeroplane

Old buildings can be knocked down by wrecking balls or blown up with explosives.

There are many different types of digger.
One type is called a backhoe loader. It has a
bucket and arm at the back and a shovel, or
loader, at the front.

Diggers can be very noisy,
so drivers wear ear defenders
to protect their ears.

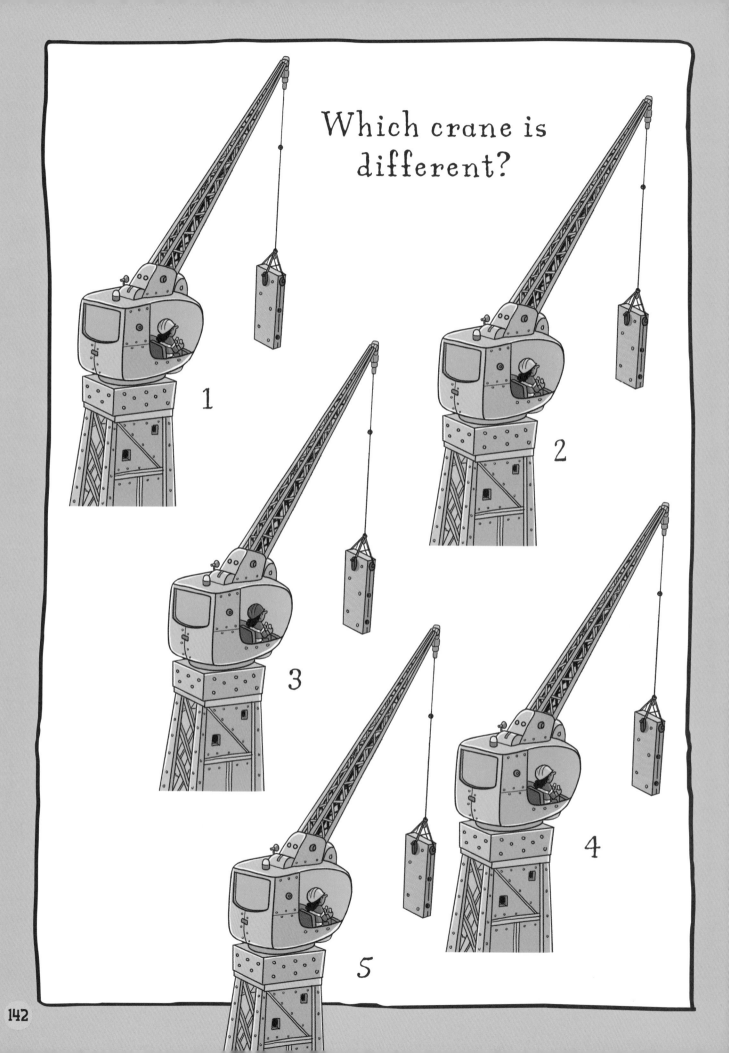

Which crane is different?

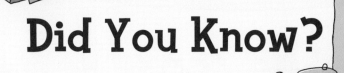

Did You Know?

The Chrysler Building, a 77-story skyscraper in New York City, was built very quickly. Four stories were completed every week.

It takes just 1.5 seconds for a 30-story building to be demolished using explosives.

The Shard in London, UK, is 309.6 metres tall and has 95 stories. The average lift speed is 6 metres per second so you can get to the top in less than a minute!

The Ancient Greeks invented cranes more than 2,000 years ago to help them build stone temples.

Who's at the Zoo?

Butterfly house

Elephants

Penguins

Gorillas

Bugs and reptiles

Aquarium

Have fun colouring in the zoo. Use lots of colours!

African plain

Big cats

Birds

Can you spot this zebra hiding among the animals in the next five zoo scenes?

Can you find and colour these things?

beetle   fish   ice cream   frog   ostrich

145

Penguins sometimes slide on their tummies!
This is called tobogganing.

Lions are the only big cats that live in groups.

149

Have fun colouring in
the birds!

Young flamingoes have grey feathers.
Colour some of them grey!

Gorillas sleep in
nests high up
in the trees.

Can you spot these things?

sun cream   boat   teapot   teddy   pitcher

155

More to Spot

Go back and find these scenes on the zoo pages!

Did you find me?

Find 10 differences between these two elephant scenes...

A Garden to Explore

Have fun colouring in all the
different parts of the garden.
Use lots of colours!

Can you spot this snail hiding in the next six scenes?

Bees

Ants

Lawn

Birds

Ants are small but strong. They work together to find food and build nests.

Can you spot these things?

earwig   daisy   centipede   trowel   seeds

Can you spot these things?

woodlouse

grasshopper

candle

crown

toy car

Caterpillars must eat as much as they can before they turn into butterflies.

Can you spot these things?

spider's web   pine cone   toadstool   green apple   red flower

Squirrels build their homes in trees using twigs and moss. A squirrel's nest is called a drey.

How many squirrels can you count?

Bees do a special dance to tell one another where the best flowers are.

169

At night the garden is still full of life. You can often see foxes playing on the grass!

Have fun colouring this night-time garden. Add a yellow glow to the lights!

Which picture is different?

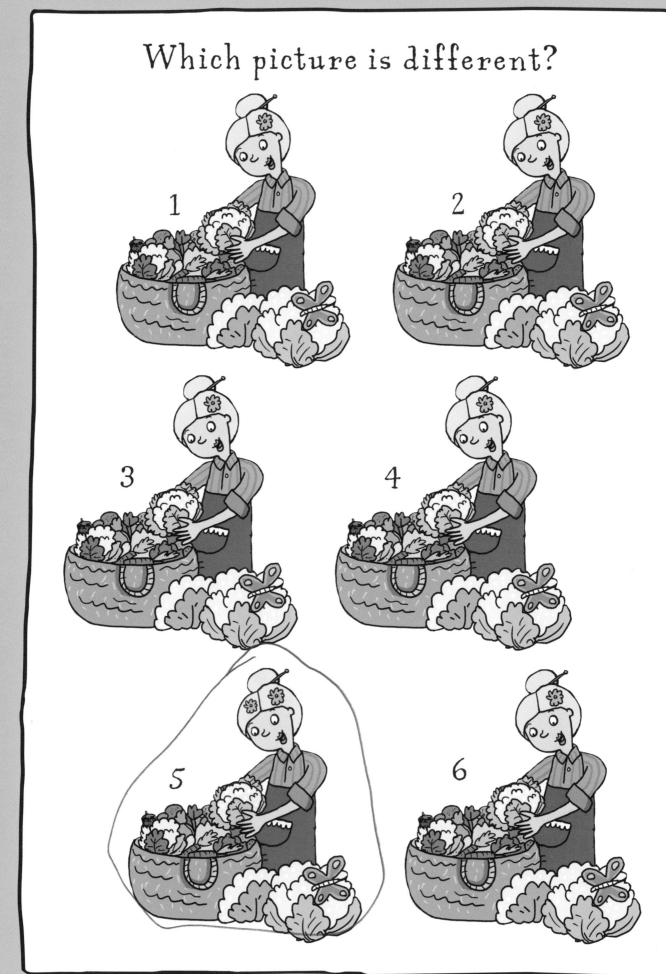

Find 10 differences between these two garden scenes...

Planet Zorgoop!

Can you find and colour these things?

house   two-headed alien   rocket   umbrella   three-eyed alien

Can you spot this robot hiding in the next six space scenes?

175

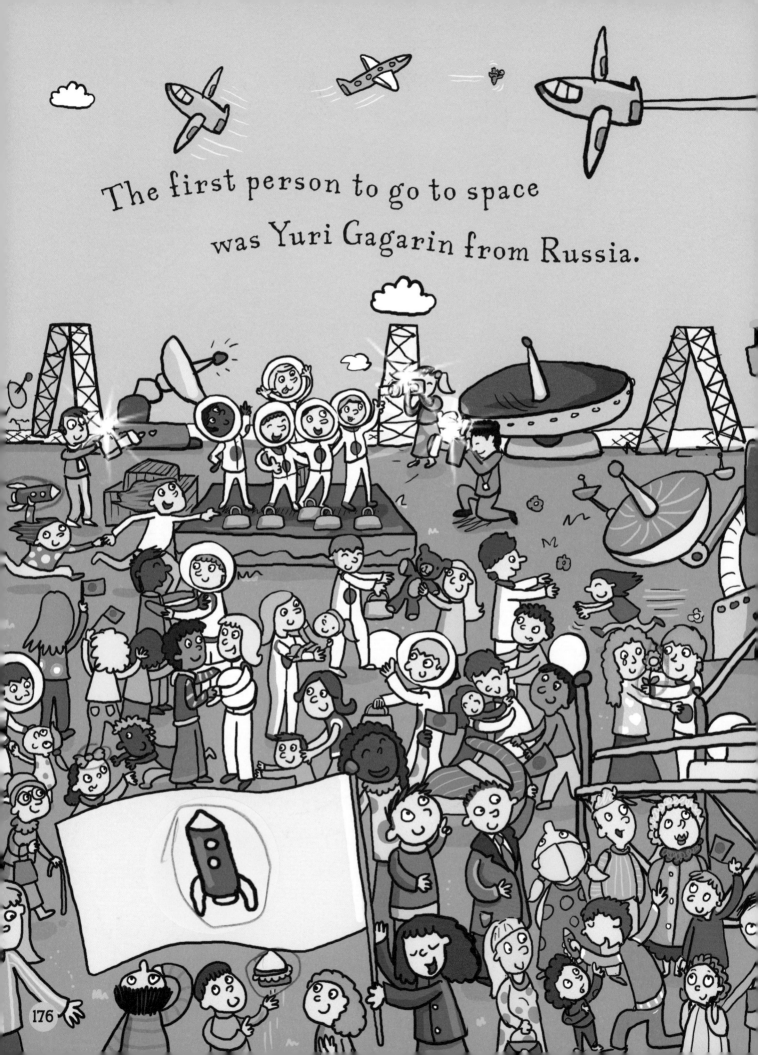

The first person to go to space was Yuri Gagarin from Russia.

177

Make your own robot!

Using an empty toilet tube, small boxes and tin foil, make your own robot. Use tape to join all the parts together and then cover them in foil. You could use stickers to add buttons, controls and a face.

Our Solar System includes the Sun
and eight planets that orbit around it.

Scientists think that astronauts will be able to land on Mars by 2040.

Can you spot these things?

dustpan

cupcake

football

ladder

flag

Can you find and colour these things?

three-eyed alien

green alien

UFO

lamp

traffic lights

Do you think aliens exist? Maybe they live in a city like this...

Welcome to Planet Zorgoop!

Which alien is different?

Find 10 differences between these two alien scenes...

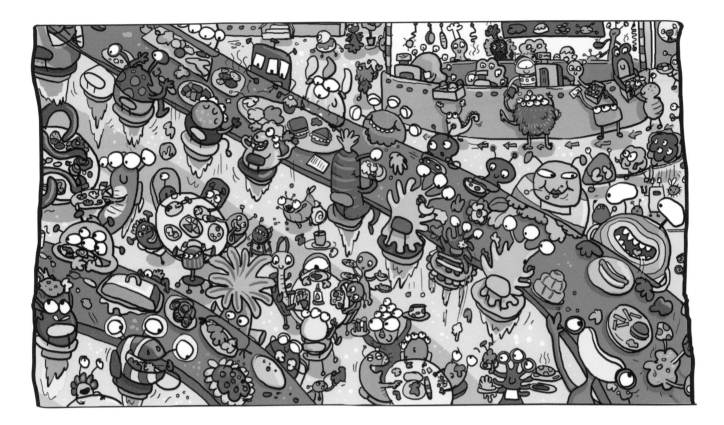

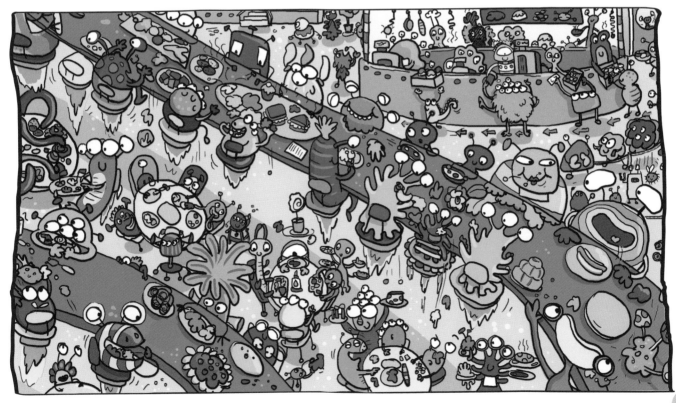

Answers

Welcome to the World!
6–7 There are four bears.

14–15
Spot the twin

18–19 There are four boats.

20 Two is the odd one out.

21
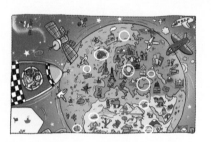

We're On the Move
24–25 There are seven yellow vehicles.

28–29 There are five dogs.

30 There are seven windows on the train.

36 Six is the odd one out.

37

Watch Out! There are Dinosaurs About
41 *Supersaurus* is eating leaves.

42–43 There are four purple dinosaurs.

44–45
Spot the twin

48 The dinosaur has four spikes on its tail.

52 Five is the odd one out.

Creatures of the Ocean
56–57 There are four divers.

62–63 There are 18 bears.

64–65

68 Five is the odd one out.

69

Step into the Jungle
72–73
Which sloth is not asleep?

74–75
Three
matching
pairs

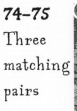 

76–77
Spot two
babies

78–79

80–81 There are eight bats.

82 Five is the odd one out.

83

Down on the Farm
88–89 There are seven ducklings.

90–91 There are four mice.

96 Four is the
odd one out.

97

Get Busy in the City
100–101
Spot the
bus stop

102–103 Ten firefighters are
wearing helmets.

104–105 There are four aeroplanes.

106–107 There are ten balloons.

108–109
Spot the
ticket
office

110–111
Spot the
toy shop